W. A. MOZART

Sonata in B flat major

KV 570

FOR PIANO

Editing & Fingering
by Victor Shevtsov

Vitta Publications

Vancouver

EDITOR'S FOREWORD

This edition of Mozart's piano sonatas reproduces the original music text based on autographs and the earliest editions. It also contains editor's fingerings, some articulation signs, added only by a comparison with authentic Mozart's indications in similar passages or phrases, and suggested dynamic marks, which are provided in small print.

Sonata in B flat major

KV 570 (Vienna, 1789)

W. A. Mozart
(1756 - 1791)

Allegro

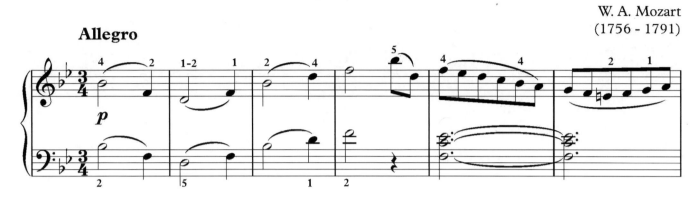

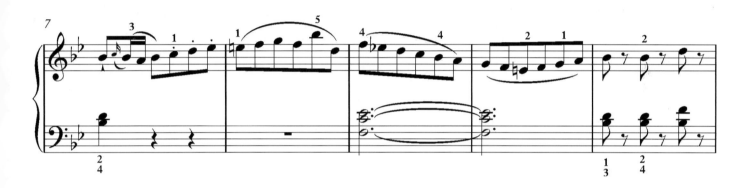

2

4

6

10

Adagio

Allegretto

Made in the USA
Monee, IL
15 February 2022

91288640R00015